H to He (I'm turning into a man)

See Primark and Die
(Buy Little Buy Less Buy Nothing At All)

Claire Dowie

I0192819

methuen | drama

LONDON • NEW YORK • OXFORD • NEW DELHI • SYDNEY

METHUEN DRAMA
Bloomsbury Publishing Plc, 50 Bedford Square, London, WC1B 3DP, UK
Bloomsbury Publishing Inc, 1359 Broadway, New York, NY 10018, USA
Bloomsbury Publishing Ireland, 29 Earlsfort Terrace, Dublin 2,
D02 AY28, Ireland

BLOOMSBURY, METHUEN DRAMA and the Methuen
Drama logo are trademarks of Bloomsbury Publishing Plc.

First published in Great Britain 2025

Cover design by Jillian Feuerstein

Cover photography by Colin Watkeys

Bloomsbury Publishing Plc does not have any control over, or responsibility
for, any third-party websites referred to or in this book. All internet addresses
given in this book were correct at the time of going to press. The author and
publisher regret any inconvenience caused if addresses have changed or sites
have ceased to exist, but can accept no responsibility for any such changes.

No rights in incidental music or songs contained in the work are hereby
granted and performance rights for any performance/presentation
whatsoever must be obtained from the respective copyright owners.

All rights whatsoever in this play are strictly reserved and application for
performance etc. should be made before rehearsals begin to Colin Watkeys,
28 Thurlow Park Road, London, SE21 8JA (c.watkeys@ntlworld.com).
No performance may be given unless a licence has been obtained.

A catalogue record for this book is available from the British Library.

A catalog record for this book is available from the Library of Congress.

ISBN: PB: 978-1-3505-8472-3
ePDF: 978-1-3505-8473-0
eBook: 978-1-3505-8474-7

Series: Modern Plays

Typeset by Mark Heslington Ltd, Scarborough, North Yorkshire

For product safety related questions contact
productsafety@bloomsbury.com.

To find out more about our authors and books visit
www.bloomsbury.com and sign up for our newsletters.

Face to Face Festival
in association with
Neil McPherson for the Finborough Theatre
presents

Claire Dowie's Swansong

Adult Child/Dead Child
Why Is John Lennon Wearing A Skirt?
Available in *Why Is John Lennon Wearing A Skirt? and other stand up theatre plays*, published by Methuen Drama.

In this volume:
H to He (I'm turning into a man)
See Primark and Die (Buy Little Buy Less Buy Nothing At All)

FINBOROUGH THEATRE

First performances at the Finborough Theatre:
Adult Child/Dead Child – 5 June 1987 and 10 June 2025
Why Is John Lennon Wearing A Skirt? – 29 January 1991 and 11 June 2025
H to He (I'm turning into a man) – 12 June 2025
See Primark and Die (Buy Little Buy Less Buy Nothing At All) – 13 June 2025

Claire Dowie's Swansong

Adult Child/Dead Child
Why Is John Lennon Wearing A Skirt?
H to He (I'm turning into a man)
See Primark and Die (Buy Little Buy Less Buy Nothing At All)

All plays written and performed by Claire Dowie.

Directed and designed by Colin Watkeys.

The approximate running time of each play is 70 minutes.

There will be no interval.

Please see front of house notices or ask an usher for an exact running time.

Please note that as latecomers cannot be admitted, performances may begin up to five minutes later than the advertised start time.

Please turn your mobile phones off – the light they emit can also be distracting.

Our patrons are respectfully reminded that, in this intimate theatre, any noise such as the rustling of programmes, food packaging or talking may distract the actors and your fellow audience members.

We regret there is no admittance or re-admittance to the auditorium whilst the performance is in progress.

Claire Dowie | Writer and Performer

Claire Dowie has a reputation for work that defies categorisation. Originally trained as a dancer, Dowie started writing poetry (published by Faber and Faber, and Apples and Snakes), and quickly gained a reputation as an outspoken and hilarious stand-up comic on the cabaret circuit of the early 1980s, before morphing into writing plays and inventing a new genre: stand up theatre. Most recently, she won the 2024 Carlo Annoni Award for a new version of *Death and Dancing*, developed at the National Theatre Studio. Other notable stand up theatre plays include *The Year of the Monkey, All Over Lovely, Easy Access (for the Boys)* and *When I Fall ... If I Fall*. Her first novel *Creating Chaos* was published by Methuen in 2004. She is currently writing a second novel, *The Dylan Deck*, and an autobiographical memoir *More of a Man Than My Mum Is* with daughter Rachel WD about growing up queer. www.clairedowie.co.uk

Colin Watkeys | Director and Designer

Colin Watkeys first booked Claire Dowie for the Finborough Cabaret in 1982. Their forty-year collaboration has created more than twenty plays and one novel. He is founder director of the Face to Face Festival and has been directing solo performers for over thirty years including Ken Campbell and Jack Klaff whose play *Kafka* he directed at the Finborough Theatre in June 2024, and which will transfer to New York City later this year. He studied philosophy in London, Japanese Theatre, Music and Dance in Tokyo, founded the Finborough Cabaret alongside Nica Burns, and worked at the Royal Court Theatre for the Young Writers Festival. Amongst his many notable productions are *Pigspurt, Jamais Vu* and *Theatre Stories* by Ken Campbell (National Theatre and Royal Court Theatre). He is currently Associate Theatre Director at Lyrici Arts in Medway. www.solotheatrefestival.co.uk

Performance Histories

Adult Child/Dead Child

Claire Dowie first performed *Adult Child/Dead Child* late night at the Finborough Theatre on 5 June 1987. It returned for a full run at the Finborough Theatre a month later, transferred to the King's Head Theatre twice, returned to the Finborough Theatre again, and then toured throughout the UK and beyond. It won a *Time Out* Theatre Award in 1988, and continues to be performed by theatre companies all over the world.

Why Is John Lennon Wearing A Skirt?

Claire Dowie premiered *Why Is John Lennon Wearing a Skirt?* at the Traverse Theatre, Edinburgh, on 14 August 1990, and subsequently at the Finborough Theatre on 29 January 1991 winning a 1991 London Fringe Award. The play was revived for the Edinburgh Festival in 2013, winning a Best of the Fest and a unique six star review in the *Edinburgh Evening News*. It continues to be performed internationally, most recently by companies in Spain (in Spanish) and India (in Marathi).

H to He (I'm turning into a man)

Claire Dowie first performed *H to He (I'm turning into a man)* at The Drill Hall on 21 October 2004. She has subsequently toured the play nationally and internationally, winning awards at festivals in Germany, Romania and Kosovo. Published in both German and Italian, there have been multiple productions in Germany and Italy, and Teatro Franco Parenti in Milan are reviving their production in Autumn 2025.

See Primark and Die (Buy Little Buy Less Buy Nothing At All)

Claire Dowie originally performed *See Primark and Die* – under its original title *Buy Little Buy Less Buy Nothing At All* – at The Drill Hall on 17 June 2010 returning in November the same year and subsequently touring the UK. The play has also been seen across Europe with productions in both German and Italian. Stage 2 Youth Theatre will present a large cast version in Birmingham in December 2025.

FINBOROUGH THEATRE

'Probably the most influential fringe theatre in the world.' *Time Out*

'Not just a theatre, but a miracle.' *Metro*

'The mighty little Finborough which, under Neil McPherson, continues to offer a mixture of neglected classics and new writing in a cannily curated mix.' Lyn Gardner, *The Stage*

'The tiny but mighty Finborough.' Ben Brantley, *The New York Times*

Founded in 1980, the multi-award-winning Finborough Theatre presents plays and music theatre, concentrated exclusively on vibrant new writing and unique rediscoveries – both in our 1868 Victorian home and online with our digital initiative – #FinboroughFrontier.

Our programme is unique – we never present work that has been seen anywhere in London during the last 25 years. Behind the scenes, we continue to discover and develop a new generation of theatre makers. Despite remaining completely unsubsidised, the Finborough Theatre has an unparalleled track record for attracting the finest talent who go on to become leading voices in British theatre. Under Artistic Director Neil McPherson, it has discovered some of the UK's most exciting new playwrights including Laura Wade, James Graham, Mike Bartlett, Jack Thorne, Athena Stevens and Anders Lustgarten, and directors including Tamara Harvey, Robert Hastie, Tom Littler, Blanche McIntyre, Kate Wasserberg and Sam Yates.

Artists working at the theatre in the 1980s included Clive Barker, Rory Bremner, Nica Burns, Kathy Burke, Ken Campbell, Jane Horrocks, Nicola Walker and Claire Dowie. In the 1990s, the Finborough Theatre first became known for new writing including Naomi Wallace's first play *The War Boys*, Rachel Weisz in David Farr's *Neville Southall's Washbag*, four plays by Anthony Neilson including *Penetrator* and *The Censor*, both of which transferred to the Royal Court Theatre, and new plays by Richard Bean, Lucinda Coxon, David Eldridge and Tony Marchant.

New writing development included the premieres of modern classics such as Mark Ravenhill's *Shopping and F***king*, Conor McPherson's *This Lime Tree Bower*, Naomi Wallace's *Slaughter City* and Martin McDonagh's *The Pillowman*.

Since 2000, new British plays have included Laura Wade's London debut *Young Emma* (commissioned by the Finborough Theatre), James Graham's London debut *Albert's Boy* with Victor Spinetti and four of his first plays, Sarah Grochala's *S27*, Athena Stevens' *Schism* which was nominated for an Olivier Award, and West End transfers for Joy Wilkinson's *Fair*, Nicholas de Jongh's *Plague Over England*, Jack Thorne's *Fanny and Faggot*, Neil McPherson's Olivier Award nominated *It Is Easy To Be Dead* and Dawn King's *Foxfinder*.

UK premieres of foreign plays have included plays by Lanford Wilson, Larry Kramer, Tennessee Williams, Suzan-Lori Parks, the English premieres of two Scots language classics by Robert McLellan, and more Canadian plays than any other theatre in Europe, with West End transfers for Frank McGuinness' *Gates of Gold* with William Gaunt, Craig Higginson's *Dream of the Dog* with Dame Janet Suzman and Jordan Tannahill's *Late Company*. In December 2022, *Pussycat in Memory of Darkness* was the first play performed by a foreign theatre in Ukraine since the Russian invasion.

Rediscoveries of neglected work – most commissioned by the Finborough Theatre – have included the first London revivals of Rolf Hochhuth's *Soldiers* and *The Representative*, both parts of Keith Dewhurst's *Lark Rise to Candleford*, *Etta Jenks* with Clarke Peters, three rediscoveries from Noël Coward, Terence Rattigan's *Variation on a Theme* with Rachael Stirling and Lennox Robinson's *Drama at Inish* with Celia Imrie and Paul O'Grady. Transfers have included Emlyn Williams' *Accolade*, John Van Druten's *London Wall* and J. B. Priestley's *Cornelius* which had a sell-out Off-Broadway run in New York City.

Music Theatre has included West End transfers for Adam Gwon's *Ordinary Days* and the UK premiere of Rodgers and Hammerstein's *State Fair*. Playlists of Finborough Theatre music theatre are available to listen to for free on Spotify.

The Finborough Theatre won the 2020 and 2022 *London Pub Theatres* Pub Theatre of the Year Award, *The Stage* Fringe Theatre of the Year Award in 2011, the Empty Space Peter Brook Award in 2010 and 2012 (and nominated in both 2023 and 2024), and was nominated for an Olivier Award in 2017 and 2019. Artistic Director Neil McPherson was awarded the Critics' Circle Special Award for Services to Theatre in 2019. It is the only non-public funded theatre ever to be awarded the Channel 4 Playwrights Scheme bursary twelve times.

www.finboroughtheatre.co.uk

Supported by

The Finborough Theatre has the support of the Peggy Ramsay Foundation / Film 4 Playwrights Awards Scheme.

Mailing
Email **admin@finboroughtheatre.co.uk** or give your details to our Box Office staff to join our free email list.

Playscripts
Many of the Finborough Theatre's plays have been published and are on sale from our website.

Sustainability
The Finborough Theatre has a 100% sustainable electricity supply, and has replaced single-use plastic glasses with paper.

Local History
The Finborough Theatre's local history website is online at
www.earlscourtlocalhistory.co.uk

The Finborough Theatre on Social Media

www.facebook.com/FinboroughTheatre

www.x.com/finborough

www.instagram.com/finboroughtheatre

www.youtube.com/@finboroughtheatre

www.tiktok.com/@finboroughtheatre

www.threads.net/@finboroughtheatre

Search 'Finborough Theatre' on Spotify

Friends of the Finborough Theatre

The Finborough Theatre is a registered charity. We receive no public funding, and rely solely on the support of our audiences.

Please do consider supporting us by joining our Friends of the Finborough Theatre scheme.

There are five categories of Friends, each offering a wide range of benefits.

Please ask any member of our staff for a leaflet.

William Terriss Friends – Anonymous. Iain Clarke. Fiona Clements. Tim Doyle. Anne and Patrick Foster. Ros and Alan Haigh. Melinda Patton. Chris Rocker. Linda Thorson.

James Bohee Friends – Janet and Leo Liebster. Catrin Evans.

Adelaide Neilson Friends – Charles Glanville. Philip G. Hooker.

Legacy Gifts – Tom Erhardt.

H to He
(I'm turning into a man)

Music: 'Simply the Best' by Tina Turner.

H *enters in blonde wig, short skirt, high heels etc. dancing
provocatively.*

I'm turning into a man.
The thought is in my head before I've even opened my eyes.
I dismiss it as the remnant of uneasy dreams and awake
fully, aware that I'm scratching. (*Right hand nails drop off as
scratching.*) I don't itch but my skin is thick and tingling,
drawing attention to itself.
I'm turning into a man.
It started with my right hand. I woke up one Monday
morning and found it attached like a limpet to my left tit.
The more I pulled the more it clung on – and I definitely
heard it say 'Oh go on, please, let me' in a distinct Brummie
accent. When it was clinging by the barest thread of a middle
finger and thumb to the end of my nipple I finally smacked
it away. 'Ouch' we both said.
It scratches around as though snuffling for truffles and is
tempted by the damper, sweatier, nooks and crannies of my
body.
It then starts wanking. Not good wanking. Fast wanking,
stumbling wanking. As though getting in five years of
fumbling adolescence in five minutes.
It wasn't pleasant, it was sore – and I only came twice.
Actually that's not bad for a man.
The hand makes a lunge for my nostrils (I am turning into a
man) my nose wrinkles in a lascivious sneer, my nostrils
widening and pulling up for maximum effect, greedily
snorting for the smell of sex, male or female, it doesn't seem
to mind. The middle finger darts in and out of my mouth,
tasting, licking, sniffing again – like a pig. I recoil, startled
by its greed. The nose and hand behaved instinctively but
they are not my instincts. Something in that movement or
that smell rekindles a mood of irritation that feels like
nostalgia, but smoky, difficult to grasp, escaping the memory
by a whisper. The hand doesn't smell like mine, but then
again, it does.

I look at it, my right hand, it's bigger than yesterday's hand, grown sometime in the night. Not grown fat, or puffy but long and thin, bony – not bad looking, quite nice.

A rash, perhaps, some kind of allergy.
I look at my left hand. In this light it looks normal, like the left hand I know and love. It also smells normal. Now I feel lopsided and uneven. (*Remove left hand nails.*) I've always gone for symmetry in my life – like matching vases, and curtains that compliment duvets.
I look again at my right hand.
It's either last night's alcohol or despair.

My nose too has turned into something else, something not my own. It's tight and tingling, as though it's got cramp, which is odd in a nose. It makes my head pound and my eyes water.

I need coffee, I'm going mad – and I need a wee.

I swing my legs out of bed. My right foot is inches bigger than my left. It has gone from a size six to approximately size nine overnight.

I am turning into a man.

I stare at the ugly monstrosity on the end of my right ankle. A long, thin, bony thing with thick wisps of black hair on the toes making the red nail varnish look comical. The beginning (or end) of athlete's foot grows between the toes. The heel skin is hard and cracked as though there isn't enough to cover and the whole foot gives the impression of unkempt grubbiness. I feel sick to look at it but mesmerised by the big toe jerking rhythmically up and down as though incessantly tapping out morse – 'stop twitching!'
It looks like a man's foot.
There is absolutely nothing attractive about a man's foot.

I feel grubby, I need a shower.
And I'm bursting for a piss.

Getting to the bathroom means negotiating three full-length wardrobe mirrors, a half-length dressing table mirror, a mirror in the hall and almost wall to wall reflection in the bathroom. I close my eyes, duck and scurry. I don't want to look at myself – don't want to look at my face. My eyesight is crashing into the unfamiliar obstruction of a very large nose. A big right hand, a big right foot and a very large nose. The rest of me, what I can see of it, seems okay. My skin is rough and pimply; goosepimply rough, but I put that down to fear. My face though. I'm frightened to look at my face. Later, perhaps, when my head stops pounding and my nerve strengthens.

In the bathroom I lift the toilet lid and the toilet seat. I pause and put the seat back down. I lift it again. That seems familiar. I put it down. That seems familiar. I try to hold and point something, but there's nothing to hold and point. My clitoris has grown though, protruding like a spectator at a window. It's no longer hooded. No longer tucked away behind my labia – my labia's grown. I'm quite well packed down there, for a girl. I try to hold the clitoris, to aim it, but it's slippery and the movement of my fingers up and down the shaft, trying to get a grip, turns into another wank – not as pleasant as you might think, while staring into a toilet bowl, busting for a piss. I give up, turn and sit. But my bladder feels squashed and uncomfortable, and I feel vaguely wussy and in need of a book or magazine. I stand to the front, sit to the back, stand to the front, sit to the back, front, back, front, back, as though the twist is my morning exercise. I've forgotten what to do. The toilet is like a stranger offering no clues and I debate sitting or standing till I give up and piss in the shower. There's a circle of piss outside the shower, where I've missed the cubicle. How could I miss the cubicle? I feel disgusted but shrug, nonchalantly.

I stand in the shower, head down, eyes closed and let the water run down my back. I'm not washing, just thinking, trying to work out how and why and what to do. Closeted in the shower stall I feel cocooned in a world of Perspex and steam and pressure powered rain. I think about crying but feel strangely aloof and more confused than upset. Then I make the mistake of turning. I catch a glimpse of myself in the taps. A fish head led by a bulbous nose. I look monstrous – as I always do in the distortion of the chrome, but the bubble of fear bursts. I lean in till my big nose burns on the hot tap. What I look like I can't tell, but there's a darkness about me that wasn't there before. Black roots are showing beneath my naturally blonde – naturally blonde! – hair. I can bear it no longer. I open the shower cubicle and stand, naked and dripping, staring at my reflection in the mirror beyond. Desperation is my immediate impression. Not ugly, not monstrous, but a stranger staring back.

I used to be blonde. I used to be blonde and blue eyed and thin and shapely and sexy and beautiful – and twenty. I used to be twenty. Sagging tits, beer belly and rugby player thighs.

As I walk towards the mirror, so the stranger walks towards me, copying every move, every blink and twitch of my body and face.

I study that face for a long time. I lean in, close to the mirror, almost kissing. My nose is actually in proportion; it's not as big as I thought it was now that I see the rest of me. My eyebrows are bushy and my eyes are . . . hazel. My blue eyes are now hazel. My eyelashes are black or still caked in last night's mascara. I rub at my eyelid; the stranger does the same. (*Remove eyelashes.*) We both inspect our fingers – no black, no colour coming off. Natural then, naturally black eyelashes. My lips are thin, my cheek bones prominent. I like this new face. It seems to know where it's going, heading for the tip of my nose. It's more angular and defined and, for the first time in my life, (*Remove wig.*) my head matches my shoulders. I look closer, much, much closer. Hair. I'm getting hair. On my chin.

Music: 'Swan Lake' by Tchaikovsky.

I phone Pam, my PA.

'Pam? I won't be in today . . .'

'Helen? Is that you?'

I hesitate at her question; it's an odd question. She sounds confused.

'Pam, can you rearrange my appointments . . .'

'Helen, what's the matter with your voice?'

My voice? I stumble through with the usual 'would you rearrange this' and 'could you cancel that?' but it's automatic. I'm distracted by my voice. I didn't think there was anything wrong with my voice.

I replace the receiver and catch a glimpse of myself in the hall mirror. I jerk my head back in surprise. I still surprise me.

'You surprise me,' I say to my reflection.

Perhaps Pam means gravelly. My voice does sound gravelly. Too much alcohol last night obviously.

'And I could kill for a cigarette.' What? I don't smoke. Strange.

'Strange,' I say.

Yes, definitely gravelly. But Pam's heard gravelly before. I debate phoning her back, but saying 'what's wrong with my voice?' ten minutes after the event sounds neurotic and might arouse her suspicions.

'Suspicions of what?' I say to the mirror.

'Of going crazy,' I lean forward and reply. I realise then I'm flirting with myself. This is ridiculous!

Music builds.

I breathe deeply and try to take stock. I look different and I'm acting strange. My cleaner will be here at nine. Do I really want my cleaner to see this?

I phone her. 'Sharon . . .'

'Helen? What's the matter with your voice?'

I phone Marion to cancel our lunch date.

'Helen? What's the matter with your voice?'

And in desperation, I phone Tina, my best friend.

'Helen? What's the matter with your . . .'
'My voice, yes. What's wrong with it?' I say.

Music cuts out.

She pauses. Then laughs. 'You've done a Thatcher, haven't you!'
'What?'
'Margaret Thatcher. You've had lessons to deepen your voice, soften the stridency.'
My turn to pause.
'Are you saying I'm strident?'
'Not anymore!' Tina cackles down the line.
I cut her off. Tina's always chirpy in the morning. I'm not. (*Starts removing tights and high heels.*)
I replace the receiver, slide down the wall and sit in a heap on the hall floor. I hug my knees, bury myself in my dressing gown and listen to Tina on the answering machine.
'Helen? Are you all right? Your voice sounds great. H?'

Tights and shoes off.

I've got Beckham knees. David not Victoria. I could've been a footballer.

I can't make a decision. I can't. My wardrobe and cupboards are stuffed full of clothes, none of which suit me, fit me or look anything other than laughable. I'd give up and go back to bed but I need cigarettes. I don't smoke but I can't face turning into a man without fags.

Maybe I should dress covered up like a nun? A nun buying cigarettes – two habits for the price of one.

Music: I Wanna Be Loved by You by Marilyn Monroe.

Comedy strip.

Then behind changing area if necessary – keep it decent! Put on old raincoat.

After a lifetime of crapness, we finally reach a point in history where it's a positive asset to be a woman – and there's

a greater choice of clothes – and I go and turn into a man!
(*Peering round change space.*) How perverse is that?

Out from changing area, then put on headscarf.

Finally decide on a big, face hiding headscarf which is a nod
to nuns but not a piss take. I thought I might look like the
queen but . . . not as common. I leave the house with bold
strides, which are intended to look confident and assertive
but only exaggerate the limp from my oversized foot.
My right leg is now longer than my left.
People are laughing. All down the road people stare at me.
Some quietly, pretending they happen to look up and there I
am. Others blatantly gawking. All laughing.
I know they're laughing even if they do wait till I've passed.
It's the limp; it draws attention to itself.

I can't do this. As soon as I enter the supermarket it seems
like everybody and everything stops. Time has stood still, all
are staring and I'm the only one shopping. They all think
the same thing: a shoplifter with no dress sense. Even the
dog tied in the doorway is barking with suspicion. A woman
'innocently' dogs my footsteps. She is quite clearly the store
detective and she's making me feel guilty. And worse, she
makes me feel ugly. My hand trembles as it reaches out to
pick up a loaf of sliced. I manhandle the soft contents in a
dirty, lascivious fashion – and this is just my left hand. My
right is buried deep in my pocket, playing with my keys and
sulking. It refuses to shop. That at least is a relief, if I was to
unleash my right hand I think someone might scream – and
it would probably be me. I drop the loaf and gravitate
towards cans of beans and convenience foods. Pot Noodles
look inviting – ten varieties, marvellous – you only have to
add boiling water and you could live on them for ever! Or
until you get rickets. I move on and pause to sneer over
Weight Watchers SlimFast One Cal low fat cholesterol
reducing strawberry flavoured yoghurt. 'We all know who
that's aimed at,' I mutter – but quietly, the store detective is
hovering. Ah Yakult. Yakult. I used to love Yakult, it was my

Bible. A lot of lovely goodness in one tiny, little bottle. And so reassuringly expensive. Yakult means nothing to me now. My life is impoverished. I move on. The detective follows. I finally decide to buy croissants. They seem the least masculine food stuff and I put them . . . no basket. I've forgotten a basket. I think about continuing but I've only got one hand, how far will I get, how much will I drop and how embarrassed will I become? I head for the exit – or rather the entrance, going back the way I came, clutching my croissants to my bosom and the store detective following. She's following! She thinks I'm going to steal. Why would I want to steal her poxy croissants when I can't even pronounce them? I turn round to glare at her, but realise store detective is actually rather attractive in an ordinary shopper kind of way. I don't know what she's wearing but it's red and shows a bit of cleavage so she's obviously dressed especially for me – I turn away, horrified by my own thoughts and almost collide with another woman. She backs off with repulsion as though I smell. I try to apologise but my gravelly voice has turned into ballast and all that comes out of my mouth is 'Sorry darlin'.' Darlin'? Also, repulsed woman strikes me as alluringly sexy. I drop the croissants and run. The dog tied in the doorway goes for my ankles but all I can think is 'Shit, no fags!' I stop running when I hit the recycling bins. I hide behind the bottle banks, and debate going back in for further humiliation and a packet of Marlboro. (The big country!) After five minutes of arguing with myself I decide to quit smoking and feel strangely exhilarated.

I have an urge to go to B&Q and look at tools. I want to mutter words like 'two-be-one' and 'grout' while writing little notes on the back of a cigarette packet with a betting shop pen. At the same time I want to look at wall tile transfers and stencilling kits. I feel my life would improve 100 per cent if I could stencil fleur de lys patterns all round my kitchen. White walls and laminate floors. Why do I keep thinking white walls and laminate floors? With a bowl of oranges, strategically placed for a pop of colour. I gravitate to the gardening section. I feel safer in gardening. I'm not bouncing from stereotype to stereotype in gardening. So long as I steer clear of shredders (dyke territory). I even start to relax, and enjoy the genderless pursuit of slug pellet comparison. Slugs? How can you tell if slugs are male or female? Are they male or female, or are they both? Or neither? I pick up a packet of swede seeds. Swede seeds. Round and reddish, and sort of womblike but definitely a male vegetable, I feel. Or are they? Swedes, are they male or female? Swedes? Tomatoes? Are tomatoes male or female? They're also red and round but more squashy and soft like a bosom – sort of bosomy – so female. But are they? Or are they male? Fat and brash and full of seed and can't make up their mind whether they're a vegetable or a fruit – so? Potatoes? (*Riffing with audience.*) Cabbages? Carrots? Long and orange – male or female? Bisexual obviously! Non binary. Sitting on the fence like a Lib Dem. Mangetout? (They're French, who cares?) Peas? Artichokes? What about broccoli? Is broccoli male or female? Obviously Italian, but Italian male or female? A drag queen! Yes, broccoli's a drag queen – big and blousy but not quite cauliflower! The genderfication of vegetables. I'm going mad . . . Or European. Or both. I think I'm safer at home.

Removes headscarf.

So, back home the door is locked, the curtains are drawn, blah's on the TV, I'm not smoking and I am doomed. My face is burning. Not painful, just hot, itchy, making me aware of things happening. The pores around my cheeks and chin have opened and wiry hair is forcing its way through. Black wiry hair. I scratch at it and hear the harsh, brittle sound of a facial scrubbing brush. Stubby hedgehogs. Men. I need a shave.

All I have is a packet of Bic razors (pink) and a dexterity untested big right hand. We're not talking teenage bum fluff – there is no practise stage.

Slaps face cream on as if shaving foam.

The occasional ring, beep, and 'Helen, are you there?' of the answering machine marks abstract, unconnected time. Pam, Tina, Marion, Sharon, word spreads, concern grows: 'Are you there?' 'Are you all right?'

Am I all right? Am I there?

I start with my legs. I know how to shave legs. From the ankle to the knee, right leg. From the ankle to the knee, left leg. Finish. Usually. But the razor has to go beyond the knee. There's hair from the knee to the groin. The razor goes from the groin to the chest, nicking the skin at the awkward curve under the breast. I stick toilet tissue where it bleeds. (*Sticks toilet tissue on face.*) I stick toilet tissue where every nick bleeds. Hair around the nipples. Hair separating the buttocks – almost perfect in its Y formation from the small of the back to the anus. Hair round the anus. Never before have the words 'back, sack and crack' sounded so meaningful. A tentative attempt with the razor under the chin. (*'Shaves' with mascara.*) A nick. Blood. (*Sticks toilet tissue repeatedly on face.*) I stick toilet tissue on it and tell the mirror I don't want to be a hairy man.

I don't want to be a man at all.
But all I get is him smirking back at me
and a body covered in toilet tissue.

I still don't feel like crying but I do lie in the bath for fifteen minutes contemplating my navel. It has gone from an 'outie' to an 'innie' overnight. My breasts have shrunk, my hips have narrowed and my bum is disappearing – my cushionless buttock bones rub uncomfortably against the enamel of the bath and the base of my spine throbs.
And all the time his big right foot rhythmically taps out its message on the bath tap.
A memory of irritation.
Somebody used to do that.
It annoyed me then, it annoys me now.

I don't want to turn into everything I hate en route to what I hate most – HIM.
He overtakes on zebra crossings.
He hogs conversations and doesn't notice.
He empathises with pregnant women but secretly thinks they're fat and ugly.
He automatically assumes he's right, just because the rest of the world says he is.

I attack.
The black fluff liberated from between the toes is enough to knit a sock. The dry skin pumice-stoned from the heel could fill a small shoe. Nails are cut, old varnish removed, toe hair depilated and exercises employed to improve the arch of the instep.

His big right foot still looks ugly.
And my left foot is beginning to look the same.

In between assaults on the foot, his big right hand caresses my shrinking breasts, explores the cave of my navel and dives between my inner thighs.
Long blonde hair floats past, sticking to the sides of the bath and twining around the soap. It is falling out in clumps. Stubby black hair grows beneath. The man emerging looks like a clueless convict – probably a body snatcher with a warped sense of humour. The rest of my hair, that which hasn't fallen out, I cut off. I don't want to look like one of those plastic bottle blondes with their roots showing through. I do have some dignity.

I retreat to my towelling dressing gown and watch TV. A bored flicking of the remote gives me blah, blah, blah, blah and . . . Eh oh! I settle down to watch Teletubbies while eating dry cereal out of the box. Every time Dipstick comes on the screen I throw a cornflake at it, I don't know why.

The doorbell rings and my breakfast jumps out of the box. My lap, the sides of the chair and the carpet are covered in cornflakes. I scoop them up and stuff them back in the box.

A cursory glance inside shows fluff, hair and strange gritty bits amongst off-coloured cornflakes. I shake the box in an effort to disperse the debris, but succeed only in bringing more to the surface. I give up, stand up, shake more crumbs from my creases and crunch across the carpet to the hall.

Whoever is at the door is peering through the letterbox. I cling close to the wall, like a thief in a strange house. I am not expecting company, nobody knows I'm home. As I skirt past the answering machine I notice the number eleven winking at me. I feel unusually popular and can't help a slight smirk of pride. My expression ruined by another pierce of the doorbell, a flap of the letterbox and those eyes again peering through.

I shimmy quickly sideways till I'm level with the door, then smack the letterbox shut with a hard downward slam.
'Ouch! Helen!' Tina yells.
She has come with concern and grapes.

Panic. I don't want to let her in. I'm getting a lump in my throat (probably an Adam's apple), and I need glasses, I can't see out of the corners of my eye.
For instance I can't see dust, and I know there is some. Yesterday the whole flat needed dusting, today it looks fine.

I tell Tina she can't come in. Tina understands but refuses to leave. I sit on the floor, back against the door, out of sight of the letterbox and guarding my territory. After a moment or two the first grape plops through the letterbox. I watch impassively as it rolls across the floor and comes to rest at the skirting. A grape is not an assault. And if it's a ploy to get me into open view of the letterbox it fails. Another grape plops through and sits on the doormat. Then nothing – silence and a grapeless letterbox. My move. I ask if the grapes are organic. There is a pause.

I imagine Tina's expression to be the same as mine: organic? Where did that come from?

But we both seem happy so Tina resumes posting at a regular and steady pace. At first I catch them – catch, chew, swallow, catch, chew, swallow – Tina and I working in the rhythm and harmony of long-standing and well-matched friends. Then I wonder how many grapes I can chew without swallowing. Then I wonder how many grapes I can get into my mouth without swallowing or chewing. Then I wonder the odds of throwing a grape up into the air and catching it in my mouth while my mouth is already full of unchewed grapes. Then I choke. More grapes plop through the letterbox as I retch a half-mashed mouthful quietly into my hand, hoping Tina doesn't hear. She doesn't seem to. Or if she does, she doesn't comment.

Her mouth appears at the letterbox.
'That's the whole bunch,' she says.
So many grapes, so little time.
'You'd better come in then,' I say.
I get up and lean my body against the door, my big right hand quarantined away from me as mushy grapes drip between my fingers. What to do, what to do. Such an awkward time to have regurgitated grapes on one's hands. I imagine Tina on the other side of the door, wondering what was wrong.

What was wrong?

I didn't want her to think there was anything wrong.

I've known Tina since I was twenty-two. She's my best friend. She was the sister of a boyfriend I used to have. Doug. I was engaged to Doug. Even supposed to marry him. But I found his sister far funnier, far more interesting, and far more comfortable to be with. So when my relationship with Doug fell apart, my friendship with Tina blossomed. I trust her with my secrets and my fears. I trust her with my life. If she doesn't accept me, nobody will. But I want more than acceptance; I want her to like what she sees. My hesitation is my fear of rejection. And, I realise, the longer I hesitate the more likely she is to reject me. I pour the mushy grapes into

my dressing gown pocket, grab my courage from between
my legs and open the door.

Tina is on her knees, her ear to the letterbox.

She looks up and gasps. 'Helen?' she says then scrambles
wildly backwards.

'What?' I say.

Removes wig cap so that hair sticks up.

I turn to look in the hall mirror. My short black hair is spiky
but rugged, my dark brown eyes sparkle, my cheekbones are
chiselled and my jaw is square. I look good. Or putting it
another way, I am good looking. My mother always said my
face was too big and my shoulders too broad to be really
pretty, but as a man I'm remarkably proportioned. And
proportion, really, is all you need in a man. I turn back and
smile. Despite galumphing backwards like a crab, Tina looks
particularly pretty today, particularly sexy.

'Tina,' I say, 'come in.'

Music: 'I Feel Love' by Donna Summer.

Tina enters my flat with the wariness of a vegetarian
entering an abattoir. I close the door behind us. 'Tina?' I say,
'know anything about testosterone?'

She doesn't.

Tina sits on the sofa and stubbornly refuses to listen.
Apparently I have brought this all on myself. Sometime
between last night and this morning I have deliberately and
secretly gone out and found a mad scientist and a plastic
surgeon and had my whole body moulded and melded,
altered and adulterated, butchered and rebuilt and injected
with transforming agent – just to annoy Tina. And, it will all
go away if we sit in silence and stare rigidly at the wall long
enough. Every time I present my cheek in her direction and
say, 'Feel it! Go on, feel that stubble!' Tina moves further
along the sofa and refuses one touch. Not one! My groin
aches.

We reach an impasse. Tina and I sit at either end of the sofa. I scratch and Tina's eyes dart with alarm in the direction of my itch.

'So, have your periods stopped?'
It's only been a day, Tina.
Silence.

Got any fags on you?
'You don't smoke.'
Sulky silence.

'What about wigs?' Tina says, with a note of triumph.

I give her a look.

'And make-up,' she says, 'lots and lots of make-up. And there must be something in your wardrobe . . .' She says as she runs screaming from the room.

Tina is going to fix me. She's going to make it all better.

I sigh deeply and put the TV back on.

Laid out on the bed like a corpse waiting for a funeral is the shortest skirt, the tightest top, the biggest bra, the fuck-me-ist shoes, and the most stupid wig I've ever had the misfortune to wear.

'I'm not twenty anymore, Tina,' I say, but Tina's not listening, she's busy rooting around my make up bag. When that fails to yield results she scoots off to root around her own.

I drop my dressing gown to the floor and, fists on hips and legs spread, I look at myself in the mirror.

Opens raincoat to reveal blank, black cloth.

Things are proceeding remarkably well. I am getting a very good body. I have no breasts and no male organs. I am flat from my neck to my knees. Neither male nor female. I am flat. I am ironed. I can be anything now, go anywhere. Pressed and dressed and raring to go. I question my lack of sentiment for my old body, wondering why I'm not sorry to see it fade. But he's coming. And he's bringing excitement with him. There's nothing exciting about my old body.

I touch my left breast. At which point Tina returns, clutching African Violet eye shadow and 1920s pan stick.

'If you've got it flaunt it,' she says, then stops.

Music cuts out.

I don't think she's referring to my body. Tina stands rigidly in the bedroom, too far in to beat a dignified retreat.

'Come and feel my breasts, Tina,' I say.

She doesn't move.

'Come on, before they disappear.'

I stare at her and myself in the mirror and scratch my left breast with deliberate exaggeration. As predicted, Tina flashes a glance in the direction of the itch.
'Touch it,' I say with more than a hint of benevolent command.

Tina's expression sets into a challenging stare. She steps forward, sticks out her index finger . . . and pokes me.

I feel like a doorbell.

'What?' she says.

'Shrinking,' I say.

Obviously the power of my body has failed to ignite her passion. She opens my hand and slaps the make-up into it before turning her back on me, my disappearing breasts, my nakedness and my lust.

Closes raincoat then cleans face.

Tina is making furtive phone calls in the hall while I watch blah on the TV. I overhear words like 'stress', 'mental breakdown', 'utter nutter'. Someone's in a bad way.

The smell of pasta sauce fills my nostrils, making my stomach rumble and my mouth salivate. Tina is making lunch. She's already made cups of tea and toast, vacuumed the living room and cleaned the mess in the bathroom. All in silence. I'm not complaining. Apart from the vacuum – I complain about the vacuum. The noise interrupts my thoughts.

Her perfume is intoxicating. Not so much for the smell as the way my senses sharpen whenever the scent announces her approach. Her clothes whisper promises of salacious delight. Her nylon encased knees and thighs create a swishing static against the satin lining of her skirt. The click of her Cuban heeled shoes on the beech wood kitchen floor. I imagine her on that floor. Imagine her tights and knickers hampering movement around her ankles, her skirt hoisted around her waist. Shoes awry, legs akimbo, lipstick smeared face, hair abandoned. A look so undignified, so unattractive as to be disgustingly sexy. None of this I mention. I feel it might alarm and spoil a perfectly good lunch.

I do think I should dress for lunch though.

(*While changing.*) What to wear, what to wear? How would she like me, what would turn her on? Jeans and a T-shirt? Trousers and shirt. Suit and tie. There's not a lot of choice. I don't have a choice – I've got nothing to wear! I'm not wardrobed for a fancied man!

I want something smart, but casual, something serious but fun. Sexy obviously – but not obviously sexy – obviously. Something 'Je ne sais quoi'. Something 'Come se dice'. Something 'Was ist los'. Something continental, European, sophisticated . . . (*Peering round change space to audience in glasses.*) And possibly glasses to make me look sensitive? Possibly not.

Music: 'Love to Love You' by Donna Summer.

H *dances, dressed in smart 'male' outfit: white shirt/black trousers/ waistcoat.*

Music continues during speech.

Tina comes to tell me lunch is ready. She looks, looks again, her eyebrows raise to her hairline. She pulls in her stomach and cheeks, and flutters her eyelashes up and down my body. There is no other explanation: Tina fancies me.

You look lovely, my darling.
'Shut up and eat your pasta.'
Perhaps a drop of bubbly with our pasta?
Shall we bubble, my darling? Shall we? Shall we bubble together? Are we a bubbly couple?
'Are you mad?'
No . . . but I think Tina is. Mad with passion, mad with desire.

I spend the whole of lunchtime flirting with Tina.
Tina flirts back, mainly by pretending to play hard to get.
She moves her chair further round the table. I follow like the Mad Hatter, madly in love with his Alice. Round and round we go in a dizzy 'dance d'amour'.

Music ends on 'doorbell'.

Sharon the cleaner arrives. Coo-ee!
I'm surprised but then remember I never got round to telling her not to come. I then get annoyed – she's supposed to be here at nine, not lunchtime.

I'm trying to seduce Tina!

'Don't mind me,' Sharon says, plugging in the vacuum, 'I've always wanted to work for a male boss.'

Male boss? Male boss?

Tina and I sit in silence as Sharon and the vacuum rattle around us. Apparently turning into a man is the sort of thing you see every day when you're a cleaner.
It's not the sort of thing Tina sees every day, though.
'Sharon? A word,' she says, gesturing Sharon to follow her to the kitchen for hurried mutterings behind the door.

They are arguing, I can hear them – words are being thrown like plates. Words like 'choice', 'freedom', twenty-first century', 'barking'.

They are fighting. Not out and out fighting, not honest fighting. But sniffy fighting, and snidey fighting. They are fighting over me. I'm flattered.

Music quick snatch: 'I Feel Good' by James Brown.

H *briefly dances.*

Sometime during coffee Tina left. I asked her to wait for the five o'clock shadow but she said I was sitting too close and she had things to do. Sharon the cleaner didn't stay either.

I knew I should have worn those glasses.

I've always washed, waxed, plucked, squeezed, buffed, pampered, painted, teased and toned. Moisturised and moisturised and moisturised. And it's come to nothing. My whole life spent pink and tingling and ready for anything. And my body turns on me, turns against me, attacks from within. Friendly fire. Like an American.

Puts on glasses.

I don't know where I am. I don't. I look into the mirror and I don't recognise myself. Everything's changed. My whole body has changed. Inside cells are forming, rushing through my blood stream and gathering, linking arms and massing in a thick picket of solidarity. I poke myself with disdain. Thick skin, foreign skin, not my own – not yet. I jab at myself the way you do with a boring lover who's taken root in your bed. 'Get out, go away, leave me alone.' I feel disconnected. Not just to myself but to the world outside. As though everything has paused and I'm the button on the video. My vision's changed. There is a circle of sight in front of me, the rest is black. But the light in front is so bright, so full of colour.

The bedroom is too pink. I've sat here now for half an hour, and, much as I've tried not to, I've been forced to conclude that the bedroom is too pink. What's disconcerting is the bedroom isn't pink. I know the bedroom isn't pink, I decorated it myself, picked the paint myself. The bedroom is Wild Mushroom with Juiced Plum trim. I know this. And yet my head sits, smugly on my neck, blowing cigarette smoke like a professional painter and decorator, and saying, 'No love, it's pink – and it's horrible.' I'm outraged. Half of me anyway, the other half agrees, it is horrible. It's pink!

Pink for a girl. Pink for a girl and blue for a boy. That's what they say, isn't it – pink for a girl, blue for a boy. So what now? What colour am I?

Three people have appeared, Old Age, Regret and Despair, sitting at a table in the corner of my living room, sipping tea. The table is covered by a white damask tablecloth, the cups are bone china, the spoons silver. They've got serviettes – just to drink tea. It's very disconcerting. There isn't room for a table in my living room.
I don't know who they are, Regret, Old Age and Despair, but they say they know me. They say I'm the chosen one. Chosen to save the world. But they say I have to change because the world isn't ready for a female messiah. I think if the world isn't ready for a female messiah, the world isn't worth saving and I tell them so. But they just laugh and pour more tea. They drink tea endlessly in the corner of my living room. They won't go away. And they never go to the toilet. It's very disconcerting. I go to the toilet constantly, I drink tea too. Sometimes I piss standing up and sometimes I pee sitting down, either way I miss the toilet bowl. I say if they want a male messiah why don't they just choose a male? They said they tried that but it got complicated. Bit of an argument, misunderstanding, slight crucifixion. They said they needed a man with female tendencies. I said why not Elton John? He's very popular – and he's got a husband. So that's like two messiahs for the price of one – a sort of heir and spare as it were. They said God and Elton John move in mysterious ways and I shouldn't question a higher authority. I told them to shove it up their arse.

I don't invite friends round anymore. The three tea sippers are my only friends. They don't let me down; they hate me no matter what I do. I like consistency. If the doorbell rings I hide behind the sofa. Well it might be Tina, and what would she say? They're such an ugly threesome – the tea sippers – and they're beginning to smell. I was never that comfortable with Tina anyway. She was always trying to prove how sexy she was . . . bitch.

I light a cigarette and the tea sippers purse their lips. They remind me this is a non-smoking household. I remind them this is my household and I am smoking. We compromise and I agree to smoke outside.
I'm six floors up and I haven't got a garden so I stand on the window ledge in the rain.
My cigarette has gone out. I try to re-light it. It won't light. It is soggy. All my cigarettes have gone soggy.
I think about jumping but . . .
I don't want to give up smoking that way.

Puts on biker boots.

I always thought my life was middle of the road and for that reason I took up pole dancing. I thought it might enhance my femininity. I cried a little, but only a little – testosterone.

I used to be young.
I used to be young and sexy and vibrant.
And I smoked too much and I drank too much.
And I stayed up till three.
And I had a bath sometimes.
And I'd plug the tap with my toe and tell myself I'm going to do something good, something interesting.
I would have a successful life.
I would be popular and sociable.
And . . . and now . . . now.

I have reached the age of visible invisibility.
I am no longer sexy or vibrant or viable.

I don't want sex, I want secateurs.
I don't want E's, I want HRT.
If I drink, it's a small white wine (because of my bladder).
If I laugh, it's a slight titter (because of my bladder).
Can I still get down and boogie though?
Yes.
Yes, I can still get down and boogie.
I just can't get up.

So . . .

Forget 'I shall wear purple'.
I will not 'go gentle into that good night'.

I am turning into a man.

Puts on leather jacket.

Slowly, day by day.
Or rather, night by night.
I wake up every morning and I'm a little bit thicker, skin wise.
I feel it as I get out of bed and scratch.
Scratch.
I never used to scratch.
I see it as I look in the mirror.
I dread looking in the mirror.
My skin crawls as I crawl – with trepidation and excitement towards the bathroom and the bathroom mirror.

My nose is bigger.
Again.

Music: 'My Life' by Shirley Bassey.

Sharon's here. Coo-ee! Has it been a week? Maybe it's been two. The vacuum, I can't bear the noise of the vacuum. I tell her to stop. I tell her I don't want a cleaner. I told her last week. I told her the week before. She doesn't listen. She says she's got to come, she's got to help because the same thing happened to her nephew. 'The same thing happened to my nephew,' she says, 'but male to female, obviously. You're lucky,' she says, 'it cost him a fortune.'

She turns off the vacuum and walks towards me.

Puts on the same blonde wig from beginning.

She treads on a cockroach.
She doesn't notice.
Only I notice.
She leans over and kisses me.
And I forget about the cockroach.
Real men don't care about cockroaches.
And I am not a cockroach.
I am a real man.

Music builds.

End.

See Primark and Die
(Buy Little Buy Less Buy Nothing At All)

Setting: a white brocade kimono stretched out on a rail upstage right. Another rail of white clothes (cheap and cheerful) upstage left.

Music: Queens of the Stone Age, 'No One Knows'.

1.

Have you ever thought you might die in Primark?
Have you ever thought you might die in Peckham Primark?
Not a thing, is it, not desirable? Because it's funny. Dying in
Peckham Primark is funny. I don't want people to laugh at
my death. It's not an ambition.

I say Peckham Primark because I've been in other Primarks
and other Primarks are like shops. People shop in them like
shops. In Peckham Primark it's like entering The Cage. A
dark, dank, low ceilinged affair, full of atmosphere and
menace and you think any minute now it's all going to kick
off so I better grab my strappy top quick before the knives
and the knuckledusters come out. Because they're scary
those fourteen-year-old girls, especially when they're in
packs.

But I like Peckham Primark. (Liked Peckham Primark.)

And don't say, 'Ugh, Primark'.
Yeah it's tat, we know it's tat. But it's cheap tat.
Why go to H&M or Gap or Monsoon or wherever where it's
expensive tat? What's the point? It's all going to fall apart by
the end of the week.

If you want not tat you've got to go to Marks and Spencer's,
where it's quality but you come out looking like a middle-
aged frump, no matter how old you were when you went in.
I saw a five-year-old go in with her mummy, ten minutes
later she came out in a twin set and pearls, sensible shoes,
carrying the Daily Telegraph. And she only went in for a
wee.

And you can always spot a Marks and Spencer shopper.
They all look like they're about to go to a slightly austere but
tastefully expensive wedding. Where they'll sit at the back
muttering criticism of the bride, and the groom, their
parents and relatives and guests, but offer up a silent prayer
of thanks to the Lord that at least the vicar has the common
decency to be white. And straight. And a man.

Not my image. I'm more cheap and cheerful and frayed at the edges.

So Primark.

The phrase 'no brainer' was started in Primark. I know because I started it. These jeans for instance. £8. I've worn these jeans for at least two years, at least (actually it's more like seven). Two years. That's £4 a year. £2 a leg. That's a no brainer. Shoes for £5. £5! Yeah, they won't last the night, but then neither will a packet of cigarettes. In fact the price of cigarettes now, it's cheaper to smoke the shoes. And probably healthier. It's a no brainer. A thong for 50p. Well . . . yes. I don't usually go for thongs but . . . Yes, it's nasty. It looks nasty. Feels nasty. Tastes nasty (don't ask, I was drunk). It's a nasty shape, a nasty colour, nasty pattern, nasty material, it looks like a hammock for a haemorrhoid but it's 50p, a no brainer. I'll have two dozen, bargain.

I went to Primark with my friend Andrea. She lives in the garden flat below me.

I wanted a long sleeved T-shirt. Red. £2.50. Bargain. Same as the brown one I bought last week. And the blue one the week before.

But I felt a bit funny when I left the flat that morning. A bit sick. Bit unsure. Almost as though I didn't want to go. Didn't want to go to Primark. Crazy. I thought it must be the weather, because Andrea said weather can do that to a person and who am I to argue.

So we got to Peckham. Parked in Morrison's. Walked around the corner. Primark looming.

It loomed.

It was too big. Too blue. The word 'Primark' leaning into my face and shouting, 'PRIMARK!'

I didn't want to go in.

Andrea said, 'Oh come on, long sleeved T-shirt. Red. £2.50. Bargain. See you in underwear if you finish before me.'

And Andrea went in.

Shiny, happy Peckham Primark. Full of characters and atmosphere. Crazed consumer bliss. People pushing and grabbing with manner-less abandon. Bras tossed into the men's section. Thongs throng the floor. Solitary shoes mourn the loss of their mate. 'Look at this! Only £6! Only four. Only two!'

I love Peckham Primark.

Loved Peckham Primark.

Broke into a cold sweat before the automatic door opened its arms to welcome me in.
Welcome to Primark. Welcome to hell.

All I wanted was a long sleeved T-shirt. Red. £2.50. Bargain. And perhaps see what else there was. Bound to be something else. Always is. And before you know it, the checkout girl says 97 quid and you think, 'what?' and you look at all the stuff you've shoved into those net basket things, half of it you can't remember what it was. And you think £97?! 'Bargain!' Think I'll go round again.

But this time I'm clinging to the rail of extra bargain, give it away, nobody wants it tat and I'm shaking. And sweating. And sobbing. And I'm dying. I'm dying in Peckham Primark. But I'm trying to die quietly because I'm dying in Peckham Primark.

I can't breathe, I'm drowning. I'm drowning in a sea of tat and I can't see Andrea anywhere. Andrea?

But suddenly this big guy appears next to me. He smiles and offers his hand. Tells me his name's Tim . . . or Jim . . . or Ted . . . or Jed. What kind of a name is Jed? Is that short for Jedediah? Bit old fashioned, isn't it? Bit biblical. Unlike

Matthew, Mark, Luke, John. Peter, Paul, Mary. Dave. Maybe
it's not short for Jedediah. Maybe it's short for Jedi?

*Music: (brief) John Williams, 'Imperial March' theme from Star
Wars.*

Bit new, bit modern. (*Calling.*) 'Come on, Jedi, come and get
your tea, come and feel the fork!'

I don't mock because his name might not be Jed, it might
just be Jim, and I'd be shouting 'Jed, Jed' and he'd say I died
in Peckham Primark calling for Jedediah. And people would
laugh and wouldn't I look a fool. So I say nothing and he
helps me out the shop and deposits me on a Peckham
Pavement.
'It's what happens,' he says. 'Be prepared. Make sure you've
got plenty in.'

Then he pats me on the head and strolls off, disappears into
the crowds.

Be prepared? Make sure you've got plenty in?

Thought it was all a bit strange.
Andrea said 'panic attack' and held up sixteen thongs and
two under-wired bras, all for under a tenner, bargain. The
thongs will match her tattoo. No brainer.

I wondered what I had to panic attack about, but didn't
discuss it because it wasn't about Andrea, and Andrea doesn't
like to discuss stuff that isn't about her.

Instead we go home discussing tattoos.

Call me old fashioned but I'm not sure about tattoos. When I
was young tattoos were for scary people like merchant
seamen or hell's angels, who had 'love' and 'hate' on their
knuckles or hearts with 'Mum' written on their biceps. That's
how you knew they were scary – they had tattoos. Now it's
women with angels on their arses and fairies on their
fannies, which is scary in a whole different way.

Andrea's got a sort of curlicue – I don't know what you call it – sort of ribbony pattern on the small of her back. And when she's not looking, I often sneak a peek at it, like bending over putting the shopping away or something. I can't help it. I stand there staring, mesmerised. Then she stands up and pffft everything goes back to normal. Weird.

2.

My Aunt Alice died. Which was a shame. I liked her. She was ninety-six, so it was expected. We'd been expecting it for about twenty years.

She was a great old lady, kept chickens and bees and grew all her own veg. She did it before it was trendy, started as a child during the war with 'Dig for Victory', and she just carried on digging.

That's where she went, in her vegetable patch, she apparently just stumbled and tumbled and fell. Her friend, Elizabeth, found her face down in a cabbage. Which is how she'd have wanted to go.

So Elizabeth decided to give her an eco-burial in a cardboard coffin, it's what she would have wanted. But we couldn't because it was too expensive. A cardboard coffin is more expensive than a normal wooden one. Because cardboard coffins have to be custom built. Custom built? *Custom built?* You could just trace round an ordinary coffin with some grease proof paper and a stubby pencil. We're talking about cardboard. Blue Peter could show us how to do it with old toilet roll holders and sticky back plastic. We could do it ourselves, just get a big box, bend her up and squash her in. Or get one of those big American fridge freezer boxes. How difficult could it be? Then we thought, yes, actually, we *could* do it ourselves. And it would be more spiritual and engaging. We could all get together, light candles, reminisce in a nice circle around the coffin. We could draw pictures or write on it, little poems or memories.

Make collages, stick a big photograph of Aunt Alice to cover up the Currys sign. Write feelings like, 'I loved you Aunt Alice, you were quietly inspirational.' Or 'Have a nice death, missing you already!' Stuff like that. We'd be much more involved and connected. It would be lovely, spiritual. Better than the usual funerals, where you sit passively while some stranger does God and Jesus for you or some happy humanist looking like a children's entertainer pretends to know someone they've never even met. And you feel desperately disengaged because it's meaningless and we're a secular society and spend Sunday mornings shopping, but we have this giant hole that we're unable to fill because we live in a capitalist, consumerist society and buying a new fridge freezer just doesn't cut it.

But at least we'd have the cardboard box to put our dearly departed in.

If you could afford it. If you were allowed to. Because it's all bureaucracy and rules.

Elizabeth wanted to throw her on the compost heap. She loved her compost heap, it's what she would have wanted. She could have carried on mulching her fruit bushes long after she'd gone. Like a legacy. Still contributing to earth, to Gaia, like a memorial, deeply spiritual. But apparently – political correctness gone mad – you have to have a certain thickness of coffin and a certain depth of burial, otherwise the foxes or rats would carry her off.
And that's a problem apparently.

Whatever happened to recycle, reuse, rethink?

Then I thought: why not feed her to the pigs? It's what she would have wanted. Aunt Alice loved pigs, she always wanted to keep them but the neighbours complained, they said it was bad enough with the chickens and bees.
Feed your nearest and dearest to the pigs, it's a great idea. Recycling. Like the Circle of Life, still involved, still contributing to the earth, to life. But it would be all nice and

civilised, tasteful, you wouldn't just throw her into the
pigpen. And you could free up cemetery space, all those
corpses rotting down, feeding the earth, making wonderful
compost for what? Grass. What a waste. And that space could
be used for building luxury apartments – you can never get
enough luxury apartments. You could make it really
spiritual with a ceremony and music and songs to the pig.
And farmers need to diversify, got to do something now that
inheritance tax is stalking them. So . . . everyone's happy. I
don't know if it would suit Jews or Muslims though. I know
they can't eat pork but can pork eat them?

But no, no, not allowed. So we had a bog-standard funeral
with a bog-standard coffin and a bog-standard vicar talking
bog-standard God and it was bog-standardly dull. Deathly –
for more than just Aunt Alice.

But on the way home, somewhere between Wigan Wallgate
and Stafford

Music: John Adams, 'Grand Pianola Music'.

I saw it. From the train. In the distance. Up ahead. A line of
washing. Looked like. Sort of. Whites. A washing line of
whites. A sheet. Couple of shirts. Socks. That sort of thing.
Looked like.

But as the train got closer. Parallel. The line of washing
changed. No longer looked like a line of washing. Looked
like a bunch. A bunch of white washing. Moulded and folded
into some kind of shape. Some kind of form.

Looked like it was dancing.

A wild dance in the wind.

Then it moved. Came closer.

At first it was outside the house. A farm house stuck in the
middle of nowhere, only seen from a train. Itself looking
spooky, like an episode of Stranger Things. But a normal
line of washing outside the house.

It was raining.

Forgotten washing.

It had rained for days.

Needless washing. Nothing desperate. Forgettable.

Then it wasn't outside the house.

When it had bunched. Formed. It moved. Danced across the fields. Danced towards the train. Almost running.

Running towards the train.

I could see that the line of washing, the bunch of washing wasn't washing. It wasn't a sheet, a couple of shirts, socks. It was clothes. White clothes. Ripped strips of white streaking behind. Streaking behind the form in the wind and the running.

Definite running. Running across and down the fields towards the train, but keeping pace, keeping its point fixed outside my window.

A figure. Human shape. Sort of. Like a black person but white. Albino aboriginal in features. Its face. Its form. Sort of. But maybe not white. Whiter than white. Translucent. Almost see-through with flowing scrappy white clothes and hair like dreadlocks, light, dancing out behind, bouncing and beating against itself.

Running outside my window. Keeping exact pace with the train. Running graceful, running easy. At the same speed as the train.

Intent. Eyes fixed ahead.

Definite human. A white black . . . man or woman? I thought man but now it seems woman. A white black woman. Translucent. Almost see-through. Keeping pace with the train.

I can't take my eyes off her.

I can't believe the ease of her running.

Intent but no effort. Determined but not desperate. Bridges don't stop her. Bushes don't bother her.

She must be on the other track. Running alongside the train on the other track. How else can she have a free run? How else can she keep pace?

Then she looks at me. First she was intent but then she turns. Turns her head and looks at me. Dead into my eyes.

I manage an 'eek'.

I manage a 'What the fu . . .'

But she smiles and runs on ahead.

Faster than the train. Smoother. Easier.

And someone touches my shoulder. I jump and turn.

'Did you see?' I say. 'Did you see?'

But the business suit puts a finger to his lips and says, 'Shh'.

'If you want to "eek", if you want to "What the fu . . ." do it somewhere else. This is the quiet carriage. Shh.'

I turn away and tremble.

I don't believe in God or ghosts, or anything like that. But I did put Jedi on the census that time. Started a new religion.

Music fades/changes to opening bars of John Williams, 'Imperial March' theme from Star Wars.

3.

Judy Bergerman.

There was an item on the 3 o'clock news, on the TV.

Judy Bergerman. Big American actress. Big as in big, not big as in famous. She's not really famous. I had to Google her.

You'd probably know her as the big American actress on the telly.

Apparently she'd been carted off to hospital, suffering from malnutrition.

They said she'd been staying at some hotel in London and she'd locked herself in, barricaded the door with a chair, trouser press, mini bar, 'do not disturb' sign.

So, after about two weeks the hotel manager thought this was odd and kicked the door down. And there was Judy Bergerman, thin. Well, thinner. And all these hotel witnesses were saying that after she'd eaten the complimentary fruit basket, she ate the complimentary flowers and then polished off the hotel stationery. And she even ate part of Gideon's Bible – Genesis to Deuteronomy. Kosher.

But then the reporter talked to a hospital spokesman who said, 'Oh yes, we're getting a lot of this sort of thing lately.' And the reporter said, 'What like anorexia . . . or bulimia . . . or?' 'No, no . . . we call it sort of shopophobia.' And the reporter went all funny and said, 'Back to the studio'.

And I thought 'What? Shopo what?' So I waited for the 4 o'clock news but Judy Bergerman was just hospitalised with a mystery illness. And by 5 o'clock she was a total has-been, not even mentioned.

4.

I started thinking about it. Because there's been a lot of weird stuff lately.
And I thought, perhaps the event on the train wasn't the ghost of Aunt Alice.
Of course it wasn't. Why would Aunt Alice appear as an albino aborigine? Running? Aunt Alice was ninety-six. She couldn't run that fast, she was built like a twig, she'd have snapped.

Perhaps the event on the train was a warning.
Perhaps Judy Bergerman was a warning.

And the incident in Primark – I went into Primark and came out with nothing. Nothing. Nobody does that, it's unheard of, it's cheapskate. And I haven't actually been shopping since. And that guy, what was his name? Jim . . . Tim . . . Ted . . . Jed? He said, 'Be prepared, make sure you've got plenty in.'

It was beginning to make sense.
I thought, I'm getting shopophobia.

I had to go to the supermarket. Judy Bergerman only had a bouquet and a Bible, I needed more than that, I had to shop like I'd never shopped before.

I didn't.
But I made a list. Be prepared.

Essentials. Necessities.

Toothpaste and toilet paper.
Before anything else, it has to be clean teeth, fresh breath and toilet paper that . . . speaks for itself.
Not literally. Not literally: 'You need a couple more wipes down here I reckon, a couple more pieces.' That'll happen soon though, talking toilet paper: 'Your arse has been wiped.' Yes, it'll be on your phone, you'll have an app for that.

Essentials. Necessities.

Food was lower on the list. In fact food wasn't on my list at all. Because what sort of food? What should I buy as a sort of last supper?
Healthy or tasty?
Because I try to stay healthy, I try to do that now.
Five a day. I do that. Five a day.
Sometimes six or seven. Once I managed eight when I had a fig roll and that's fruit. Well actually it was a packet of fig rolls – you can't just eat one – so super healthy.

When did that happen? When did I start doing what government advisors told me to do? Five a day, and lower your cholesterol, and alcohol units. When did I start believing what they said?

Puddings, alcohol, cigarettes. That's what I used to do. Stodge and booze and nicotine. And I used to feel great. Loved my life. Now it's all be healthy and fit for life. The NHS can't cope. It needs people to die. Old people and smokers are supposed to die. The NHS was paid for by smokers. It's what propped it up. Since people have stopped smoking the National Health Service is falling apart at the seams. Mainly by treating all the ex-smokers who are still alive who should be dead by now.

And I'm one of them. I should be dead, the amount I smoked and drank. Instead I'm eating satsumas and doing yoga.

It doesn't make me happier. All this health and fitness doesn't make us better people. Doesn't make us happier because our bowel movements are regular. Eating fruit and vegetables and exercising and getting fit and giving up smoking and lowering our cholesterol and going out and stabbing people and sitting in our cars raging at the world and shouting 'Get out of my fucking way!'
We're not happy. We're healthy and miserable. Bring back the good old days when we all had rickets and a sense of humour. At least then you could get a parking space.

And everybody suddenly needs their own personal toilet, so they can hide in it and cry about their miserable and shitty lives. Everything is en suite and extra toilet now. I've seen it on Grand Designs. Upstairs toilet, downstairs toilet, inside toilet, outside toilet, family toilet, guest toilet, compost toilet, chemical toilet, toilet in every bedroom. We have to have toilets dotted everywhere because of all the fruit and veg we eat, we can't go further than three feet. And that's what all the room fresheners are for, Glade and Ambi Pur and Febreze, and those ones that sense when someone's farted and give a little squirt of freshness to cover it up. The whole of capitalism is about shit and covering up the smell of it. We'll have mobile toilets soon, another app to add to the collection.

And two of everything. Now that we've got everything, we've got to have everything again. Two of everything. Not just two toilets, but two kids, two cars, two mortgages, two jobs, double oven, even though nobody cooks, double dip recession, two heat sources – central heating and a wood burning stove just in case global warming's not warm enough for you. We even have to have two bins for our rubbish. It's like some crazy Noah's ark thing but in reverse. We're all drowning in the two by two sea of stuff we buy.

The shopping list. So far I've got toothpaste and toilet paper. But do I really need them?

People used to use old newspaper in toilets. When I was a kid, for instance, my Aunt Alice had an outside toilet and she would cut the Daily Mail into squares, nice neat, same size. Very house-proud, my Aunt Alice, and ever so slightly fascist in her own little way. Then she stuck them on a bent up nail, so you could read little snippets about the evils of immigration and you either agreed with the Daily Mail or you wiped your arse with it. Either way everybody was happy. Toilet paper cost little in those days. Costs a fortune now. Velvet, quilted, double quilted, four-ply, eight-ply, like a duvet. Super absorbent multi-million pound industry. And now they're embossed. With little flowers. Why? And infused. Infused with something or other, aloe vera probably. The whole country is infused with aloe vera. Or jojoba, mango and avocado, chamomile and cucumber, lemon grass and couscous, you never get baked bean smell do you? No, because toilet paper is aspirational. You might be useless, but as long as your arse is on the up and up . . .

And toothpaste. Do I really need that? Somebody said bicarbonate of soda. But I'm not sure about that, I mean what is it? Can I grow it? Can I make it myself?

No. Salt. And I can get free salt anywhere. Individual little sachets from KFC, McDonald's, Burger King, all those fast food places, anywhere. Free. Even Marks and Spencer's café in Croydon. Not ordinary salt of course, not from M and S, oh no. Marks and Spencer's is rare extra virgin rock salt, probably pink or purple, hewn from the tomb of Joseph of Aramathea and extra finely ground by a marble pestle on the bald head of a Tibetan monk. Far, far better class of salt.

I cleaned one half of my teeth in Marks and Spencer salt and the other half in McDonald's salt. The Marks and Spencer teeth definitely look better, privately educated, almost French.

So my list of essentials, toothpaste and toilet paper – isn't essential after all.

If I am getting shopophobic, I want to do it like Judy Bergerman – barricade myself in and see what happens . . .

I ran out of milk, drank black coffee. Ran out of coffee, drank tea. Then water. Ran out of bread, ate cake, then stale cream crackers left over from Christmas.

It was as simple as that, and infinitely easier than giving up smoking. And it actually felt good. Like a weight had been lifted.

Even when I was down to a last jar smear of Marmite and an old pickled gherkin I didn't feel desperate or panicked. I was calm, almost Zen-like.

I suppose I knew at the back of my mind I could always go to the shops. I live in London, I'm surrounded by them. I knew I had a choice of either death or Tesco's. It wasn't like people in Sub-Saharan Africa who have to walk three days to get to their local branch.

I've got the Co-op on the corner of my road, Iceland a bit further up. Sainsbury's practically next to that, Tesco's opposite and another Co-op just along from that.

If I don't fancy supermarkets I've got grocers. Outdoor grocers, indoor grocers, Greek grocer, Asian grocer, Jamaican grocer, Turkish grocer, Polish grocer, Indian grocer, African grocer. There's Kentucky Fried Chicken, Dallas Chicken, Maryland Chicken, Tennessee Chicken, Morley's Chicken, Chicken Shack chicken, Subway, fish and chips, Chinese takeaway, Indian takeaway, pizza, pasta, kebabs, Bagel Bar, Thai restaurant, Caribbean restaurant, Japanese sushi bar, organic deli, vegetarian café and a French market on Fridays if I fancy Brie and a baguette.

And if I need more choice I can pop on a bus to Brixton.

Mucis: John Williams, 'Grand Pianola Music'.

Just get up and go.

But go where?

Which supermarket? Which shop? Where should I go when or if I finally go? I want to be connected to my shop. I want it to mean something. I want some depth to this life. I want the shop to reflect my image, I want it to be spiritual – symbiosis, connectivity.

I can't go to Iceland because mums go to Iceland.
Don't want to do Asda because I hate . . . (*Pat bottom à la Asda ad.*)
If I was average and conventional I'd go to Tesco.
If I was average and conventional and northern I'd go to Morrison's.
But I don't want to be average and conventional. Northern or southern.

If I liked Jamie Oliver I'd go to Sainsbury's but even he doesn't go to Sainsbury's anymore, so if it's not good enough for Jamie Oliver it's not good enough for me.
If I was middle class and rushed off my feet, ferrying Jeremy and Jemima to ballet classes and piano lessons and pony club and I haven't time to cook unless everything's prepared and half cooked already I'd go to Marks and Spencer's.

If I was very rich and aspirationally neurotic and wanted my cucumbers to colour co-ordinate with my condiments I'd go to Waitrose.

But none of these fit. They're not me. So what sort of shopper am I?

I've got a feeling I'm a Lidl's shopper. Lidl's with aspirations towards Aldi's.

As I said, cheap and cheerful and frayed at the edges.

Music fades.

5.

In the end I went down to Andrea's flat. Knocked on her door, said 'Andrea, I'm starving.'
She invited me in, commented on how well my new diet was going, then produced a six pack of doughnuts, with a yellow sticker and the word 'Reduced' on them.

Exactly how I felt. Reduced.

Just like Judy Bergerman.

But I couldn't have managed without Andrea. She saved my life. She was amazing, dropped in every day, just to see how I was doing, sometimes twice a day. And she always brought a packet of biscuits, or crisps, or a cake.

But we started to resent each other. Her, because she was feeding me all this food, and me, because I thought she was trying to ruin my diet – even though I wasn't on one. So we had a little chat, a little cry, a DMC, and we moved onto a more formal footing. She bought the food, and I went down to hers to prepare and cook for both of us and clear up afterwards. Seemed fair and we both benefited.

And it was nice. We became really good friends and enjoyed each other's company.

In fact I practically moved in with Andrea and Andrea practically let me.

She even came back from work one time to find me digging up her garden. She asked what I was doing I said, 'Making lunch – eventually.' But what I was really doing was turning into Aunt Alice.

I wanted chickens and bees and allotments . . .

I wanted row upon row of fat nutritious vegetables. But all I got was row upon row of fat nutritious slugs and snails.

What to do? What did you do, Aunt Alice? I can't buy slug pellets. And even if I could I wouldn't, because I can't stand seeing them writhing in agony. It goes on for hours, it's cruel. I watched them once, they were saying, 'Oh God, I've eaten something, I don't know what it was but it was blue.' Andrea and I thought about cooking them, like escargot . . . But . . . nah.
So I collected them in a bucket – every night, hundreds of them. At first I'd release them in the front garden next to the South Circular Road, hoping they'd see a green car and think it was speeding lettuce. But they just turned up in the back garden again the next day. I don't know how because we live in terraced houses. They'd have had to ring the bell and ask to be let through. But I had a bike by then so I took them to Belair Park, then Dulwich Park and finally Sydenham Hill Woods, where they seemed to stay.
And the few that return I use salt. Mostly McDonald's or KFC where they go Shshllpp. (*A slug suddenly dehydrating.*) And occasionally I use Marks and Spencer salt, and they go 'Sacre Bleu!' Shshllpp. (*Dehydrating in French.*)
And the veg garden thrived.
And so did we.

Till Andrea got ill.

She was in bed with something nasty. There was no food in her flat, there was no food in my flat, it was spring there was no veg so . . .

I had to go shopping.

Music: Muse, 'Exogenesis Part 1'.

The sky darkened as fat black clouds scudded across the ether and meshed into one giant portent of doom. From somewhere a fox barked a lonely warning. An old witch cackled (might have been Andrea). And the door creaked open to reveal the South Circular Road car-less, lifeless, save for the hoot of a startled owl, the screech of a lovelorn cat and the moan of wizened, misshapen old trees casting black sinister shapes amid the white fog of foreboding, their gnarled finger-like branches pointing ominously in the direction of Tesco's.

Music stops suddenly.

Tesco? Oh no, I won't go to Tesco. No, no, I well remember Dame Shirley Porter, the owner of Tesco in the eighties or nineties – don't remember that well – gerrymandering Westminster to keep the Tories happy at the expense of the poor. I think she's dead now, but no, still won't go to Tesco. Besides the Co-op is closer.

So I grabbed an umbrella and set forth, lurching down to the Co-op. I made it to the door but couldn't go in.

Nothing had changed. Shops stayed the same – closed to me.

Every automatic door brought out a sweat. Every push your own proved too much. Every pull was a pull too far. I shuffled along the High Street, alternating between a hot sweat and a cold sweat, a shiver and a shudder, a cry and a curse, and a 'Hi. All right? How's it going?' to the neighbours and friends that I passed.

It was hopeless. Andrea was ill and I was useless. After all she's done for me and I can't do one little thing for her. I hate myself, I hate my situation, I hate this shopophobia and I hate my life.

I headed for the cemetery. It seemed right under the circumstances when stuck in Norwood High Street with nowhere to go but down.

But the rain lifted, the clouds parted, a sun beam shafted onto the canvas cover of the outdoor grocery stall – more a barrow than a shop.

Vegetables and fruit shone a smile of welcome.

'You can buy us,' they whispered, 'we're okay, we're outdoor, organic, non corporate, family run, barely eeking a living, you'd be doing us a favour, a worthy cause.'

A tingle ran down my spine. I wanted to believe. I wanted to bring back health to Andrea. But a shadow fell across my face, I turned. There he was again, that man, what was his name – Ben or Ken or Roy or Troy? Anyway he handed me a bunch of overripe bananas and a slightly squashed cake and said mystically, 'dumpster diving'. Which is mystical American for going through the bins.

How low do I have to go? What kind of an illness is this?

But Andrea was intrigued.

As soon as she was better, Andrea jumped out of bed, snapped on a pair of Marigolds and off she went.

So, since I was a little bit in love with her . . . so did I.

There is something more scary than recession, old age, terrorism, third world war, tariffs and Trump, and spiders. Sell-by dates.

People are terrified of sell-by dates. They think sell-by dates will kill them, they think they'll explode.

They must do because supermarket bins are full of them. Full of food on or near its sell-by date. And slightly bruised apples, and carrots that just need peeling, squashed bread, slightly dented tins, potatoes that have lost their plastic bags.

Me and Andrea ate like kings. We had a field day. We had a field week. A field month. We could have had a field year but the supermarkets padlocked their bins.

The supermarkets locked up their bins.

To stop the food escaping.

Perhaps this is why people are terrified of sell-by dates. Or perhaps it's genetically modified food. The Daily Mail called it Frankenstein food. Perhaps for once they were right.

When genetically modified food hits its sell-by date perhaps it becomes undead, zombie food.

Perhaps the zombie apocalypse is undead food wreaking havoc on the country – on the planet. A soft banana tunnelling its way out and terrorising West Hampstead. A tuna and sweetcorn sandwich attacking old ladies in Ladbroke Grove. A day old baguette holding up a bank in the city and demanding money with menaces.

It was either that or the supermarkets were just being churlish.

Locking up their rubbish so we can't take what nobody else wants.

So I put on my best Aunt Alice voice and marched in to complain.
I can only complain as Aunt Alice. I'm rubbish complaining myself, nobody takes a Brummie seriously. Including myself. ('This is broken.' 'No it's not.' 'Okay, sorry.')
Aunt Alice asked to speak to the manager. The manager said it was orders from above.
'What? God?'
'No, Head Office. We've had a memo. Apparently there's been a lot of this sort of thing lately, all over the country.'

And I thought of Judy Bergerman.

This means there are more than just me and her. This means there must be people up and down the country suffering from shopophobia and going through bins. This means there's probably loads of us. There's probably hundreds, thousands. This means I'm finally trendy.

6.

I bumped into Roy or Troy or Bez or Jez in Brockwell Park. I said there's more than me and Judy Bergerman. He said 'Of course there are, there are thousands, that's why pubs are closing, that's why High Streets are shutting down, but it will never be reported. They say it's the internet but . . . You'll never be on the news or in the papers, because it's scary. They're terrified. But if you want to meet others . . .' And he gave me a place to be and a time to be there, to meet others, other shopophobics.

Ten o'clock in the morning in a nightclub in Soho. I was expecting a sad circle of social misfits, all emaciated and smelly. But it was like a nightclub at 10 o'clock at night. Hundreds of people, all dancing and partying and getting rat-arsed on homemade scrumpy which someone had brought barrels of.

Music: Ray Bryant, 'Madison Time' (part 2 instrumental).

We danced and drank and chatted, exchanging information and hints and tips and stories and help.

And every time a record stopped a man yelled 'I'm a plumber if anyone needs me.'
Which is not a thing I thought I'd ever hear in my lifetime.

Somebody asked me if I knew what fiscal rules were. I thought it was some sort of Australian football thing.
Somebody else asked what toxic debt was.
I knew this one. It's a Britney Spears song. I requested it.

And we danced.

A group in the corner were having a big debate about whether standing orders and direct debits was cheating. I thought 'Oh for heaven's sakes!' How can it be cheating if it's a disease? Does a diabetic cheat with insulin? Is penicillin a crime? There's always a group of fanatics, always in the corner, always taking groups too seriously and too far!

And the rest of us danced.
And we talked.
And somebody mentioned Saliki.

Music: John Adams, 'Grand Pianola Music'.

And I said 'Who?'
Saliki.
Everybody's seen Saliki.

Sometimes she's a man, sometimes a woman, sometimes an animal. Sometimes she's a line of washing. I saw her from a train. Others did too. People have seen her on motorways. She likes to run. She likes to race. She's fast. Like the wind racing through the country, or maybe even the world.

And one time we were talking about Star Wars. And it turned out we'd all put Jedi on the census that time. Started a new religion. Maybe this was it. So if anybody else put Jedi, be prepared if you're not already, make sure you've got plenty in, because you will meet Tim or Jim or . . .

Everybody knows him but nobody knows his name. So we decided to call him Jesus. A) because it's memorable, nobody's going to forget the name Jesus. And B) it doesn't rhyme with anything, Jesus/Besus/Mesus – it doesn't rhyme. And he might be Jesus. He might be the messiah. Might be all things to all men. Or he might just be a chronic mumbler. We don't know, we don't care, we're Jedi, we just feel the force and carry on dancing.

Music: back to 'Madison Time'.

And it's great being shopophobic. I've been like this for years and I love it. At first it was horrible; felt my world was falling apart. But I've met loads of people and we help each other, we have lots of friends now who have different talents that we can share, or swap.

And I've had a lot of help from Andrea. Couldn't have done it without her, she's been brilliant. We live together now like two crazy old ladies. We keep chickens and bees and grow our own fruit and veg, and we've got allotments. Just like Aunt Alice and her friend, Elizabeth. Digging for victory. Andrea's not shopophobic, she's what we call a 'freegan' and she rides around on her bike, in a coat made out of recycled crisp packets. All those cyclists you see around now, hundreds of them, they're pretty much all shopophobics or freegans. We are slowly taking over, though not necessarily in a nice way.

And Andrea spends her time going from bin to bin, and salvaging things we could use.

Music: fades.

She saw Keir Starmer going through the bins in Westminster. Rachel Reeves was keeping look out. So I now know what fiscal rules means: only one person allowed in any one bin at any one time. All that trouble Starmer got in taking all those freebies and whatnot – he had to, he's shopophobic, that's why he looks like a constipated geography teacher – it happens to all sorts.

But shopophobia, what is it?
I still don't know.
Some think it's political, some think it's an illness, some think evolution, some think revolution, some think it's a new religion.
I don't know.
I don't know what to think.

The only thing I know is this pair of jeans – £8 – a no brainer.
A long sleeved T-shirt. Red. £2.50. Bargain.

But going through the bins with Andrea?

Priceless.

Fade out.

The End.